Treasure of the Heart

Written by
Peggy Palmer

Illustrated by
Rosemarie Gillen

Halo
PUBLISHING
INTERNATIONAL

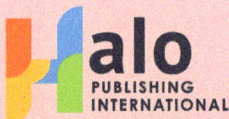

Halo Publishing International
7550 WIH-10 #800, PMB 2069,
San Antonio, TX 78229

First Edition, September 2023
ISBN: 978-1-63765-445-3
Library of Congress Control Number: 2023911698

Halo Publishing International is a self-publishing company that publishes adult fiction and non-fiction, children's literature, self-help, spiritual, and faith-based books. Do you have a book idea you would like us to consider publishing? Please visit www.halopublishing.com for more information.

I am honored to dedicate this book to Joe, Allyse, Tony, and Dawyne. I am thankful for continued inspiration from my brother, Johnny, Aunt Linda, Uncle Mikey, Aunt Rene, and my lifelong friend, Kimmy. I also want to give thanks to my family friends Stacy, Andrew, Chelsea, Anooj, Sidney, Dan, Calum, and Jerrod.

A portion of the proceeds will directly benefit Peggy's Promise, my personal mission. Out of abundance, I will give.

"Mom, if our most important treasure is in our hearts, why does my race, hair color, skin color, or anything on my outside make me…me?" Joey asks.

"Because every little thing about you makes you, you," Mom replies.

Joey thinks about it and then asks, "But why focus on the differences on the outside—like my browner skin, my darker and curlier hair—when our hearts and love are the same?"

"Your inside and outside are wonderful parts of you because you are a treasure," Mom says. "It's so important that you love ALL of yourself, and then you can share your love with the people around you. Being beautifully different is something to be proud of."

Mom says with a beaming smile, "Let's think about the hearts of your friends. If we find the love from the inside out, we'll find the real treasure."

kindness   curiosity

Joey says, "Yes! We can celebrate our differences and love our friends for everything they are. We can gather the good of their hearts and let them know we all matter. Love, that's who we all are."

"Time to explore and collect treasures of the heart!" Joey says excitedly.

Mom adds, **"We need to listen carefully with our hearts and minds."**

"Come on, Boo, want to go on a treasure hunt?" Joey asks.

Boo wiggles his little tail and replies with a joyful bark.

"When I find a treasure, I'll clap my hands and say, 'YES! I found a treasure!' Does that sound fun?" Joey asks.

Mom claps her hands and says, "YES! I found a treasure—your curiosity and kindness for what others have in their hearts, Joey."

Joey claps his hands and smiles.

YES! I found a treasure!

1. Curiosity + Kindness = Love

Joey suggests, "How about my friend Dan? We both like to write, so we wrote a story together for school. He is a treasure because we like the same things. Dan helps me feel like I'm not alone."

Mom agrees, "Yes, remember when we went on vacation, and Dan took Boo to his house? He loves Boo too. He's a good friend to you both."

Joey claps his hands and smiles.

YES! I found a treasure!

2. Friendship = Love

Mom says, "Jerrod is a good friend too, right?"

Joey describes his friend Jerrod by saying, "Yeah, we like to swim and play freeze tag in the backyard. We just love to be outside and moving. Jerrod makes my heart feel good because we get to exercise and talk. We can grow to be strong. Even though I'm not great at outside stuff, he accepts me as I am, and we still have a good time. Just like Jerrod says, 'Start where you are, and we'll have fun.' **He said he feels like a part of our family because we all welcome him with open arms. He says being open is important, and I agree.**"

Joey claps his hands and smiles.

YES! I found a treasure!

3. Acceptance = Love

Celebrating differences

Joey says loudly, "Sidney, Ally, and I like to sing and dance together, and we share lots of good music energy. We are all beautifully different, and we have a lot of fun together. Sidney always says she brings Black-girl magic, Ally brings bubbly, White-girl charm, and I bring my Latino fire as I dance the salsa. Sidney says she loves hugs, so we always show her she's loved by hugging her."

Joey claps his hands and smiles.

YES! I found a treasure!

4. Celebrating Differences = Love

"Chelsea is more comfortable observing and cheering us on. She likes supporting us, admires our talent, and makes us all feel loved. We are all happy that it makes her happy to watch and clap for us; she is right where she belongs."

Joey claps his hands and smiles.

YES! I found a treasure!

5. Belonging = Love

Mom asks Joey, "I wonder what treasure you gather from your little sister, Ally, and brother, Tony?"

"Sister Ally is sunshine. And just being next to her, I know she loves me, even though we tease each other sometimes." Joey smiles. "She creates her doodles with love. It makes me think she'll be a great artist when she grows up," Joey says.

Joey claps his hands and smiles.

YES! I found a treasure!

6. Art = Love

"I love watching movies. Maybe I'll be in the movies when I grow up," Joey continues. "Tony might look a little like me, but he is very different; he loves to take things apart and fix things. I think, when he grows up, he will help people fix their cars and houses. He'll make people feel safe, and he'll be helpful."

Joey claps his hands and smiles.

YES! I found a treasure!

7. Helping Hands + Safety = Love

Mom explains, "Cousin Calum calls his mom Mum because he lives in a different country—Scotland. His mum said he thinks differently than us, so if he's playing with toys while we talk, that helps him focus."

Joey says, "I'm happy to play with my cousin. He is gifted, can solve puzzles, and is good with video games; we can learn from him."

Joey claps his hands and smiles.

YES! I found a treasure!

8. Celebrating Different Minds = Love

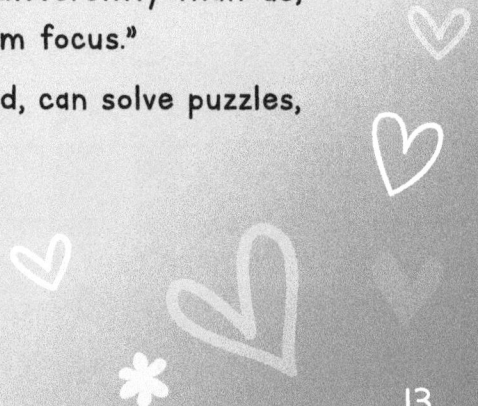

Smile

Amor

Joey says, "Our friend Andrew is good with words. Andrew also likes to tell jokes that make us all smile. Even Ally, who sometimes rolls her eyes, can't help smiling. **I like collecting those smiles and keeping them in my heart."**

Joey claps his hands and smiles.

YES! I found a treasure!

9. Smiles = Love

Joey continues, "I tasted buttered tortillas, tamales, yellow rice, and beans for the first time with Andrew and his abuela. Mom, that's what he calls his grandma. The food was so good! Can we try and make it for dinner sometime?"

Mom nods yes.

"Andrew was in a school play where they all spoke Spanish. Andrew knows more Spanish words than I do, even though we are both Latino. I like to hear him talk. I also I like to hear people from all over the world speak."

Joey claps his hands and smiles.

YES! I found a treasure!

10. Spanish Language = Amor

11. Latin American Food = Love

Joy

Respect Boundaries

Laughter

Joey says, "Even if Anooj and Ally are going through a day that doesn't go their way, like if it's scary or sad, they can always make each other laugh. They laugh so hard that it makes me laugh too. It's fun, and I gather joy in my heart."

Joey claps his hands and smiles.

YES! I found a treasure!

12. Joy + Laughter = Love

Joey remembers something and says, "But Anooj can be serious too. One day we were talking about how we were all different. Anooj asked if we could all share something about ourselves that doesn't have to do with differences? Could WE just BE together?"

Mom replies, "Anooj is a good friend, giving you kids space and **a place just to be yourselves is so important.**"

"Yeah, and now I show respect and ask my friends what they want to share. I tell them it can be about anything. And I ask what I can share with them," Joe says.

Joey claps his hands and smiles.

YES! I found a treasure!

13. Boundaries + Respect = Love

GATHER THE GOOD

"Our treasure hunt was fun!" Joey says.

"Wow, Joey." Mom smiles. "You've talked about thinking differently, making people feel safe, feeling like you belong, and remembering to love yourself. How did you get so smart with your heart at your young age?"

"Mom, we just need to embrace differences, be kind to everyone, and gather the treasures of the heart. Love is what you've been teaching us our whole lives," Joey says.

Mom adds, "Even if we have a moment when we aren't very nice, we can apologize and promise to do better. Being kindhearted is something we can all practice and learn to do."

"Friends always remember how we make them feel, so let's give them good memories," Joey adds.

"Yes, Joey," Mom replies. "I love the way you and your friends support each other with fun times by sharing food, movies, music, and toys."

Respect

You Are Loved

Celebrating differences

Friendship

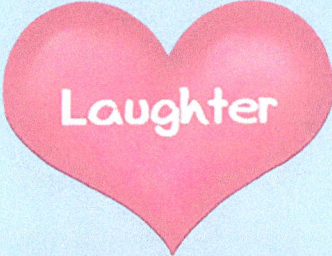

Laughter

Acceptance

Amor

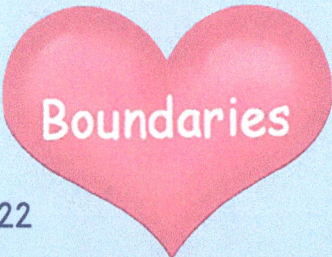

Boundaries

Helping Hands

Mom asks, "Joey, is how we make people feel really the most important work our hearts can do?"

Joey smiles and says, "If we can celebrate differences, find each other's gifts and treasures, we'll be happier in our lives. I know that because I listened to you, my teachers, and my friends."

Mom says, "I love the way you think. When people feel loved, respected, and cared for, that's the greatest treasure we can give to the world."

Helping others feel loved and cared for is our gift to the world.